VIVIENNE FRANZMANN

Plays include *Bodies* (Royal Court,   *Snow*
Queen (Bristol Old Vic, 2016); *Pest*   *...eak*; Royal
Exchange, Manchester; Royal Court, 2014); *The Witness* (Royal
Court, 2012); *Mogadishu* (Royal Exchange; Lyric
Hammersmith, London, 2010).

Awards include the Bruntwood Prize for Playwriting, 2008; the
George Devine Award for Most Promising Playwright, 2010;
and a BAFTA for short film *Lizard Girl*, 2014.

Vivienne has taught playwriting nationally and internationally.

Other Original Plays for Young People to Perform from Nick Hern Books

100 Christopher Heimann, Neil Monaghan, Diene Petterle

BANANA BOYS Evan Placey

BOYS Ella Hickson

BRAINSTORM Ned Glasier, Emily Lim and Company Three

BROKEN BISCUITS Tom Wells

BUNNY Jack Thorne

BURYING YOUR BROTHER IN THE PAVEMENT
Jack Thorne

CHAOS Laura Lomas

COCKROACH Sam Holcroft

COMMENT IS FREE James Fritz

THE DOMINO EFFECT AND OTHER PLAYS Fin Kennedy

THE FALL James Fritz

GIRLS LIKE THAT Evan Placey

HOLLOWAY JONES Evan Placey

MOTH Declan Greene

THE MYSTAE Nick Whitby

OVERSPILL Ali Taylor

PRONOUN Evan Placey

SAME Deborah Bruce

THE SMALL HOURS Katherine Soper

START SWIMMING James Fritz

STUFF Tom Wells

THE URBAN GIRL'S GUIDE TO CAMPING AND OTHER PLAYS Fin Kennedy

THE WARDROBE Sam Holcroft

WHEN THEY GO LOW Natalie Mitchell

Platform

Platform is a series of plays for young actors with all or mainly female casts, which put young women and their stories at the heart of the action – commissioned by Tonic Theatre, published and licensed by Nick Hern Books.

BRIGHT. YOUNG. THINGS. Georgia Christou

HEAVY WEATHER Lizzie Nunnery

THE GLOVE THIEF Beth Flintoff

THE LIGHT BURNS BLUE Silva Semerciyan

RED Somalia Seaton

SECOND PERSON NARRATIVE Jemma Kennedy

THIS CHANGES EVERYTHING Joel Horwood

For more information, visit www.tonictheatre-platform.co.uk

Vivienne Franzmann

THE IT

NICK HERN BOOKS

London

www.nickhernbooks.co.uk

A Nick Hern Book

The IT first published in Great Britain in 2021 as a paperback original by Nick Hern Books Limited, The Glasshouse, 49a Goldhawk Road, London W12 8QP

The IT copyright © 2021 Vivienne Franzmann

Vivienne Franzmann has asserted her right to be identified as the author of this work

Cover image: Photography by Ekua King; Design and art direction by National Theatre Graphic Design Studio

Designed and typeset by Nick Hern Books, London
Printed in Great Britain by Mimeo Ltd, Huntingdon, Cambridgeshire PE29 6XX

A CIP catalogue record for this book is available from the British Library

ISBN   978 1 83904 037 5

There are many people who have contributed to the development of this play.

Thank you to Ola Animashawun, Emily Lim, Polly Findlay, Abigail Graham and everyone on the Connections Team at the National Theatre.

Thank you to all the actors who took part in the readings at the Lyric Theatre and at the National.

Thank you to all the youth leaders, teachers and facilitators who chose the play to stage as part of the Connections Festival.

And, of course, thank you to all the young actors who discussed and performed the piece with such enthusiasm, curiosity and commitment.

V.F.

The IT was performed as part of the 2021 National Theatre Connections Festival by youth theatres across the UK, including a performance at the National Theatre.

Each year the National Theatre asks ten writers to create new plays to be performed by young theatre companies all over the country. From Scotland to Cornwall and Northern Ireland to Norfolk, Connections celebrates great new writing for the stage – and the energy, commitment and talent of young theatremakers.

www.nationaltheatre.org.uk/connections

Characters

GRACE FREEMANTLE
CHORUS
STUDENTS
MUM
DAD
SAM
BARRISTER
MS JARVIS
NEWSREADER
LOCAL MOTHER
SUPPLY TEACHER

Note on Play

The are thirty-two speaking parts. Feel free to multi-role.

The Chorus is a minimum of five people. No maximum.

The Chorus represents all the information that Grace sees and hears.

Members of the Chorus take on the roles of Mum, Barrister, etc.

The song that is referred to in the pizza scene, the classroom scene and penultimate scene can be any song you think fits.

The CHORUS *makes its presence felt.*

The CHORUS *buzzes. It fizzes. It hums. It is here.*

*

STUDENT 1. She was quiet.

STUDENT 2. Yeah.

STUDENT 1. Didn't really notice her.

STUDENT 2. Nah.

STUDENT 1. Not shy exactly.

STUDENT 2. No, not shy.

STUDENT 1. But not loud either.

STUDENT 2. No, not loud.

STUDENT 1. The sort of person that if someone at school said 'You know Grace?', you'd say 'Who's Grace?'

STUDENT 2. 'Who's Grace?'

STUDENT 1. And they'd say Grace Freemantle.

STUDENT 2. Grace Freemantle.

STUDENT 1. And you'd say, 'Who's Grace Freemantle?'

STUDENT 2. Exactly.

STUDENT 1. And they'd say, 'She's the one in 11F.'

STUDENT 2. The one in 11F.

STUDENT 1. And you'd say, 'Oh, the one with the hair and the glasses.' And they'd say, 'No, that's Miriam.'

STUDENT 2. That's Miriam.

STUDENT 1. And then after a few tries, you'd get it.

STUDENT 2. Yeah.

STUDENT 1. You'd remember who she was. You know the sort, not that good-looking.

STUDENT 2. Nah.

STUDENT 1. Not bad-looking though.

STUDENT 2. Nah.

STUDENT 1. Not clever. Like clever clever.

STUDENT 2. Nah.

STUDENT 1. You know, not in the top sets or anything like that.

STUDENT 2. Nothing like that.

STUDENT 1. But not the bottom sets either.

STUDENT 2. Nope.

STUDENT 1. Not a joker.

STUDENT 2. Nah.

STUDENT 1. Or a troublemaker.

STUDENT 2. Nah

STUDENT 1. Or a loner.

STUDENT 2. Nope.

STUDENT 1. She had friends.

STUDENT 2. Yeah, she had friends.

STUDENT 1. They weren't popular.

STUDENT 2. Unpopular.

STUDENT 1. No, not unpopular.

STUDENT 2. No, yeah, no, yeah, not unpopular.

STUDENT 1. Grace was just kind of…

Beat.

STUDENT 1. You know those American kids that go into high schools and shoot everyone dead? And the teachers go, 'No big surprise, he hasn't spoken for two years, he's been wearing the same black sweatshirt for eleven months and his chemistry book is full of drawings of guns.'

Beat.

Well, Grace wasn't like that.

STUDENT 2. She wasn't like that.

STUDENT 1. She was average.

STUDENT 2. Yeah, average.

STUDENT 1. Grace Freemantle was totally average.

STUDENT 2. Totally average.

GRACE. I am Grace Freemantle. I was totally average.

CHORUS *buzzes.*

*

STUDENT 3. My dad is mates with Grace's dad Matt. My dad always says Matt is 'a good bloke'. My dad's a twitcher, which means he's a birdwatcher. Yeah, cringe. Totally. I hear you. Matt, Grace's dad, is also a twitcher. The pair of them go down the marshes every Sunday with their binoculars and then they go for a fry-up at Despina's Café and chat about sparrows and bob-tailed tits. That's a real bird. That's its real name.

Last year, Matt, Grace's dad, posted this video of Grace having a tantrum when she was little.

CHORUS. Forty-six likes. Fifteen thumbs-up. Twenty-seven tears-of-laughter emojis.

GRACE. I am five years old. I am wearing my 'Little Miss Sunshine' T-shirt. Dad is playing with his new phone. We're supposed to be going to the park. I ask him. He says he's busy. But he promised. Before, he promised. And that is not fair.

STUDENT 3. It is a funny video. I can't deny that. She's screaming on the floor, little arms and legs all over the place.

GRACE. I am fire and fury inside.

STUDENT 3. Then she gets up and she falls onto her Lego. And if you've ever fallen on Lego, you'll know that it hurts like hell. And Grace's dad, Matt, films it all on his new phone, giggling away. Not in a horrible way, just, you know, like a dad way.

GRACE. I am red and blood and pus inside.

STUDENT 3. Grace's mum, Jen, comes in to see what's going on. She tries to reason with Grace, but there's no point.

GRACE. I am blast and yellow and clash inside.

STUDENT 3. Jen tries to cuddle her and Grace kicks her.

GRACE. I am rupture and burst and storm inside.

STUDENT 3. And Matt, Grace's dad, says:

STUDENT 3 *and* MATT. 'Your behaviour is completely inappropriate for a young lady.'

STUDENT 3. And Grace roars in his face. Like actually roars. Like properly roars. And she's sent to her bedroom to think about what she has done. And Jen turns to Matt and says, 'What did we do to deserve her?' and they burst out laughing. And the video stops.

Matt found the video last year and he put it up on Facebook with the title 'EPIC Dis-Grace'. Which is kind of funny and clever because it's a pun on her name, Grace. Dis-Grace. Epic Dis-Grace. But also a bit, you know, crap of him. All the parents thought it was hilarious, my dad included.

CHORUS. Comments.
    Epic. Dis-Grace. Lol. Emoji thumbs-up
    Little Miss Sunshine. Lol.
    Give me that over a teenager any day.
    Preach. Emoji fist-bump.
    The roar! Emoji love-heart eyes.
    Yes! The roar! The roar! Five emoji love-heart eyes.

FYI. I'm not saying that Matt, Grace's dad, posting that video on Facebook has got anything to do with Grace and that day in PE and what happened and everything. I mean it probably didn't. It's just, you know, I wouldn't like it if my dad did that. It's not a very responsible adult grown-up thing to do.

*

GRACE. It's December. Cold. Evening. Seven o'clock. I am at home. My dad is still at work. Mum has just got back from her shift and is eating a sandwich with some chutney she found at the back of the cupboard.

I am in my bedroom, staring at my GCSE revision timetable. My revision timetable is colour-coded and covered in fluorescent Post-its that Dad nicked from work. My parents are big on revision and working hard and me being the 'best possible version' of myself. My revision timetable is a work of art.

Mum takes a bite of her sandwich and shouts up the stairs:

MUM. Grace, are you revising?

GRACE. I like the way the pink and the yellow Post-its look next to each other.

MUM. Grace, did you hear me?

GRACE. They remind me of sweets.

MUM. Grace?

GRACE. Like rhubarb-and-custards.

MUM. I hope you're revising, Grace.

GRACE. Like the rhubarb-and-custards I had when we went to the seaside when I was seven.

MUM. It's maths and physics tonight, isn't it?

GRACE. When we walked along the beach and found shells and Dad ran into the sea and I had a '99' ice cream and Mum ruffled my hair and snuck a bite of my Flake, but I didn't mind cos the sun was shining and the sea was wavy.

MUM. Grace, I'm not going to nag you. Remember, it's your future.

GRACE. And that's when I first feel it.

MUM *and* CHORUS. Your future.

GRACE. In my belly. I feel…

MUM *and* CHORUS. Your future.

GRACE. A presence.
    A gnawing.
    A squirming.
    It is small.
    Like a cherry pip.
    Or a baby shrimp.
    It is really small.
    Whatever it is.
    But it's here.
    It's definitely here.

*

STUDENT 4. Grace Freemantle?

—

Grace Freemantle in PE?

—

More like Grace Freemental.

—

Grace Free-mental?

—

D'you get it?

—

You don't get it.

*

SAM. I met Grace on my first day at primary. We were best friends. We are best friends... were... are... I dunno... it's hard to... since... Anyway, I loved primary. We all loved primary. Every Thursday, our teacher, Mrs Drake, took the whole class onto the school field and told us to look up at the sky. She told us about cumulus clouds and stratus clouds and nimbus clouds. She asked us to close our eyes and listen to the music of the wind in the trees. She asked us to lie on our stomachs and feel the heat of the earth on our skin and look at the grass and count all the different things we could see. She said, 'Isn't the world a wonderful place?' And we nodded, belly down on the hot soil. One Thursday, I counted nineteen things in the grass. Grace counted nineteen too. We both saw an iridescent bug with bright-green wings. It was beautiful. I miss being seven. I miss counting interesting things in the grass.

*

GRACE. I am in the library. I am reading a book about... I don't know what it's about, because I'm not reading it really. It's for English and it's boring and I'd rather read my own books than the books that someone else tells me I have to read. I flick through Insta on my phone.

CHORUS. A young woman stands in a bikini on a beach.

GRACE. My insides feel hot.

CHORUS. A young woman stands in a bikini on a beach. The beautiful orange sun sets behind her.

GRACE. I feel...

CHORUS. The palm trees are a vivid green.

GRACE. My stomach feels wormy.

CHORUS. She is tanned.

GRACE. Like the night before an exam.

CHORUS. The orange sun makes her glow.

GRACE. Or when your friends don't respond to your post.

CHORUS. Her body is slim and curvy.

GRACE. Or when a teacher says, 'Can I speak to you after class?'

CHORUS. Her bikini is the brightest white.

GRACE. It is pulsing in my body.

CHORUS. Her hair is windswept and natural.

GRACE. I can feel it pulsing in my body.

CHORUS. She is having the best time.

GRACE. Pulse.

CHORUS. Post. Didn't want to leave our little place at @clearwateribiza today.

GRACE. Pulse.

CHORUS. Thank you to everyone @clearwateribiza for such a gorgeous two days… Emoji waves.

GRACE. I'm not pregnant if that's what you think.

CHORUS. Emoji sun, emoji pink hearts times two.

GRACE. I've never had sex. Never been near any sperm.

CHORUS. Emoji white hands preach. Hashtag Ditsy Bikinis.

GRACE. And it's not another Jesus, just to be clear.

CHORUS. Hashtag Seawater Shampoo.

GRACE. I don't know what it is, but it's not that.

CHORUS. Hashtag easyJet.

GRACE. Pulse.

*

STUDENT 5. Grace Freemantle was a normal person. Until she wasn't.

*

GRACE. There's a special school assembly with a special guest. The special guest is a famous barrister who went to the private school across town, which has its own theatre and a cricket pitch and ancient oak trees. Our school doesn't have its own theatre or cricket pitch or ancient oak trees. Our school has one-between-two books and teachers who go off sick. The barrister is very passionate.

BARRISTER. I want you to look around you. I want you to look to your left. Now look to your right.

Beat.

Welcome to your competition.

GRACE. My womb contracts.

BARRISTER. You will sit your GCSEs at the same time. You will sit your A levels together. You will apply for university at the same time.

GRACE. My womb judders.

BARRISTER. And what I want to know is what are you doing to stand out from everyone here?

GRACE. It expands in my womb.

BARRISTER. You are at a crucial point in your lives.

GRACE. It expands.

BARRISTER. Every choice you make now will impact on your future.

GRACE. It grows to the size of a chestnut.

BARRISTER. Let's get real here, do you want to own your own house? Well, how are you going to get it?

GRACE. It's not painful. But not not painful either. It feels sort of…

BARRISTER. How are you going to manage that? Because houses are expensive.

GRACE. Unknowable.

BARRISTER. You should be thinking about the things you want in the future now. What is your plan?

GRACE. It feels like the worst is yet to come.

BARRISTER. What is your five-year plan?

GRACE. Or the best is yet to come.

BARRISTER. You are in charge of your destiny.

GRACE. It grows to the size of a mouse.

BARRISTER. With hard work and determination you can make your dreams come true.

GRACE. It grows to the size of a hamster.

BARRISTER. Harness your power.

GRACE. By the end of the assembly, it is the size of a newborn puppy.

BARRISTER. You can make it happen.

GRACE. A small one.

BARRISTER. The hard work starts now.

GRACE. A Jack Russell maybe.

BARRISTER. The competition started yesterday.

GRACE. Or a West Highland Terrier.

BARRISTER. Welcome to the real world.

GRACE. Yes, like a West Highland Terrier puppy scrabbling around inside me.

*

STUDENT 6. My memory of Grace Freemantle before that day in PE, before it happened is kinda hazy… She was in a couple of my classes and yeah… nothing much really… just kind of… no nothing… Oh yeah! Actually, no that wasn't her… Oh, yeah, I remember something! There was this one time, right? It was break and me and my lot were by the art block. My mate Al was laughing and looking at his phone. And I said, 'What's that?' and Al passed it over. Someone had posted a video of Riley Miller, who's in the year below, winning the hundred-metre sprint in the borough championships.

Just so you know, a bit of context and that, Riley Miller was the fastest runner in our school. She was, like, superhuman. She broke all the running records all the time. She was in the local paper and some famous coach came from Manchester specially to see her and there was some chat about the next Olympics.

Anyway, so in the video, Riley Miller is running this race for the school in the borough championships, really fast, obviously. And in the video, you can see quite clearly that Riley isn't wearing a sports bra. She's just got her normal bra on and her boobs are really bouncing and cos she's so fast and her boobs are big, they're flying all over the place. And someone has put up a title that doesn't say 'Superhuman Woman Slays All the Competition in the Borough Championships'. Instead they've written 'The Fastest Tits in the Borough'.

And all my lot are creasing. I don't think it's funny but I don't want to seem... I dunno... I sort of half-laugh because... I don't want to... Anyway, Grace Freemantle walks by and Al shows it to her. Grace looks.

CHORUS. Fastest Tits in the Borough! Six hundred and nine tears-of-laughter faces. A hundred and ten green sick faces. Forty-two thumbs-up. Thirty-seven aubergines.

She doesn't say anything, but doesn't laugh either. She gives the phone back to Al and goes into her art class. (*Pause*.) I told my form tutor about that video cos I thought an adult should know what was going on, but I don't know if he did anything. And that's my Grace story. Sorry, it's a bit of an anticlimax, isn't it? (*Beat*.) Riley refused to come to school after that. Yeah, it's more of a Riley story than a Grace story. Sorry. Yeah. Sorry.

*

GRACE. When it is asleep, it throbs in time with my heartbeat.
It's like we're one thing.

I know we are not one thing.

It plays around.

Sometimes I think it has feathers. Sometimes I think it has fur.
Sometimes spikes like a porcupine. It wrestles and tumbles
inside my body. I can feel its spine up against my kidneys.

*

STUDENT 7. It was February when I first noticed Grace being
a freak. My mum had just got engaged to Scott, aka The
Dickhead. She was trying to get me on side so she'd given
me ten quid to get some dinner as a treat.

Me and Grace was in Pizza Town waiting for our pizzas.
Mine, an extra-hot Hawaiian with olives, cos I'm half-Italian
and I love pineapple, so sue me. Grace was having a
margherita. Classic. Pizza Town is not a place that is
bothered about cleanliness. The tables are bare sticky and the
floor... you don't want to think too hard about that. Let's just
say the mop is a stranger to that floor, but the pizzas are
banging, so swings and roundabouts, innit. There's this TV
in the corner, right up by the ceiling. It's not a flat-screen, it's
one of those old ones with a big bum at the back. Some bare
boring news was on. Grace was watching it.

CHORUS. There are children and women and men in an
inflatable boat on the sea. The waves are enormous. The boat
is sinking.

GRACE. It scuttles down from my belly, across my pelvis and
into my thigh.

STUDENT 7. The sound was off. Ed Sheeran was blaring out at
a million decibels making the news look like the most
boringest music video ever.

CHORUS *sings a line/lines from the song.*

STUDENT 7. And Grace just kept watching.

CHORUS. A woman slips from the boat. She has a baby in her arms. She tries to keep the baby above her head as she is dragged into the water.

GRACE. Its body quivers inside my thigh.

STUDENT 7. Mum met The Dickhead through her mate Kash who used to go out with him but dumped him because he was 'high maintenance'. When I met him, I didn't like him one bit. He was cold to me when Mum went out the room and a bit nasty to her when she didn't do what he wanted.

CHORUS. A terrified man reaches for the screaming baby and passes it to a terrified teenage girl.

GRACE. It pushes its tiny skull up against my kneecap.

STUDENT 7. I tried to say something about it to Mum, like, 'Look at the warning signs,' but she said, 'Don't you want me to be happy?' And there's nothing you can say to that and then she gave me ten quid. So, there we was, in Pizza Town, waiting. Me, worrying about my mum and The Dickhead, and Grace staring at the TV like she'd never seen a TV before.

CHORUS. The woman disappears under a crash of foam and bubble.

STUDENT 7. I said, 'Grace, what are you going to do next year?'

GRACE. It taps at my kneecap. Tap.

STUDENT 7. I said, 'Are you going to stay on at school?'

GRACE. Tap. I put my hand above my knee. I massage the skin. I try to soothe it.

STUDENT 7. I said, 'Grace?' (Beat.) 'Grace!'

CHORUS. The boat upturns. The children, women and men scream and shout. They cling to the inflatable, which grows soft under their touch.

GRACE. My leg violently jerks, hits the underneath of the table.

STUDENT 7. And you'll never believe what happened next. She just got up and left. She left me in Pizza Town without even a goodbye. I'm like are you joking? Are you actually joking? Who does that? She weren't even my first choice to get pizza with. I only asked her cos everyone else was busy.

GRACE. I crouch behind the bins out the back. I take a deep breath. I look at my leg. Just above my knee, it is straining against my skin. I can see the outline of its face. There's a beak. It has a beak and it is straining against my skin.

STUDENT 7. My mum went ahead and married that dickhead.

*

STUDENT 8. Grace was in my maths class. I liked her. I think she liked me too. Sometimes she'd catch me looking at her and she'd smile over at me. And sometimes I'd catch her looking at me and I'd smile over at her. There was something between us, I could feel it. You can, can't you? You can feel it when there's something there. I was going to ask her if she wanted to go out somewhere or come over to mine or whatever. But then she changed and I didn't. (*Beat.*) I wish I'd… She was nice… I really wish I'd… I wish I'd said to her, 'You can talk to me if you want. No pressure. I'm here if you need to talk.' I wish I'd done that.

*

STUDENT 9. We were in geography.

STUDENT 10. It was proper boring.

STUDENT 11. Grace was sat on our table.

STUDENT 9. Seating plan.

STUDENT 10. Between – (*Points at the other two.*)

STUDENT 9. The teacher, Ms Jarvis, loves a seating plan.

STUDENT 10. Ms Jarvis is scary.

STUDENT 9. Innit, the way her eyes bulge out of her head when she's annoyed.

STUDENT 11. That lesson, Ms Jarvis was going on about carbon emissions

STUDENT 10. Ms Jarvis is always going on about carbon emissions.

STUDENT 9. Ms Jarvis really hates carbon emissions.

GRACE. It is asleep. It is curled around my heart.

MS JARVIS. It's important to understand that the earth's climate is changing at an unprecedented speed.

GRACE. It wakes up.

STUDENT 9. I don't even know what a carbon emission is. (*To* 10 *and* 11.) Do you?

STUDENTS 10 *and* 11. Yeah.

STUDENT 9. Oh.

MS JARVIS. We can see this in higher temperatures all over the world along with rising sea levels.

GRACE. It wants something.

STUDENT 9. Geography isn't my thing. Art is my thing.

STUDENT 10. You're sick at art.

STUDENT 9. Thanks hun.

MS JARVIS. We can see this in more frequent and severe floods.

GRACE. I don't know what it wants.

STUDENT 11. Ms Jarvis was droning on so I got my phone out to show the others this bag I liked. I passed my phone to Grace under the table.

CHORUS. annabeauty, one-point-one million followers. This beautiful clutch makes the perfect travel bag! And it's only £42.99.

MS JARVIS. We can see this in more frequent droughts and storms.

STUDENT 9. Grace looked at the phone really close. I remember cos I wanted to see it, but I couldn't get to it.

CHORUS. annabeauty. Hashtag clutch, hashtag retro vibes, hashtag bring on the summer!

MS JARVIS. We can see this is the loss of habitats and the animal population.

STUDENT 10. Grace was gripping the phone like – (*Does it.*)

STUDENT 9 (*laughs*). Yeah, like – (*Does it.*)

CHORUS. PixieDream22. annabeauty, I want your bag!! I want your life!!

MS JARVIS. It's estimated that in a hundred years more than fifty per cent of species could be extinct.

GRACE. Its body tenses.

STUDENT 10. She had her head right down like – (*Does it.*)

STUDENT 9 (*laughs*). Like – (*Does it.*)

MS JARVIS. And once we have lost these animals, there is no going back.

STUDENT 9. And Grace suddenly looked up.

STUDENT 11. But she was still gripping my phone like – (*Does it.*)

GRACE. It scuttles along the length of my torso.

STUDENT 11. And I wanted my phone.

MS JARVIS. Climate change is a catastrophe in waiting. For all of us.

GRACE. Its body bristles.

STUDENT 9. Yeah, cos here if the teachers see your phone, they take it.

MS JARVIS. And the consequences for humans can already be seen.

GRACE. It starts climbing up my ribcage.

STUDENT 10. Yeah, they lock your phone in a safe.

MS JARVIS. Around the world we see crop failure and starvation.

GRACE. It pulls itself up inside my ribcage. I think it has teeth.

STUDENT 9. And your mum or dad or older sister or whoever has to come and collect it.

MS JARVIS. Around the world we see desertification and forced migration.

STUDENT 10. My dad had to come and get my phone. He was livid.

MS JARVIS. And this is only going to get worse.

GRACE. There's a noise.

STUDENT 11. I really wanted to get my phone off of her before Ms Jarvis saw it.

GRACE. There's a noise inside of me.

MS JARVIS. We have ten years to do something before catastrophe is inevitable.

STUDENT 11. So I reached over and I grabbed it out of Grace's hand.

GRACE. I can hear it inside me.

MS JARVIS. Just ten years.

STUDENT 10. Yeah, that's when she went really weird.

STUDENT 11. It wasn't my fault.

STUDENT 10. Not saying it was.

STUDENT 11. Oh, I thought you were.

STUDENT 10. It was no one's fault. Or it might have been somebody's fault, but we don't know, do we?

GRACE. I can hear it from inside me.

STUDENT 9. Then Grace leaned right over the desk and held her stomach. Like – (*Does it*.)

STUDENT 11 *and* 10. Yeah.

MS JARVIS. Ten years for global leaders to take action.

STUDENT 10. And I said, 'What's up, Grace?'

MS JARVIS. And my question to you is...

GRACE. It's making this noise like –

MS JARVIS. What can you do about it?

STUDENT 11. And I said, 'Grace are you alright?'

MS JARVIS. Does anyone have any ideas?

GRACE. I pull my jumper round me so no one can else can hear.

STUDENT 9. And then Grace did a very unGrace thing.

GRACE. I don't know how to stop it from –

STUDENT 11. Very unGrace.

GRACE. I can't make it –

STUDENT 10. Totally unGrace.

GRACE. They're gonna hear.

STUDENT 9. She started –

GRACE. They're all gonna hear.

STUDENT 11. Yeah, she started – (*Laughs*.)

GRACE. I can't let them hear it.

STUDENT 10. She started – (*Laughs*.) singing.

GRACE *sings quietly some Ed Sheeran song/or any other you think is better for this moment, but should be the same as the one in the pizza scene and penultimate scene.*

MS JARVIS. What on earth is –

STUDENT 9. And it was proper funny seeing Ms Jarvis's eyes popping out all over the place, so I – (*Sings.*)

MS JARVIS. Why are you –

STUDENT 10. And me. (*Sings.*)

MS JARVIS. I'm warning you –

STUDENT 11. Until we were all – (*Sings.*)

They sing.

MS JARVIS. Stop it!

They sing.

Stop this right now!

They sing.

I said stop!

They stop and burst out laughing.

STUDENT 11. And that's when we realised.

GRACE. And that's when I realise.

STUDENTS 9 *and* 10. Yeah, we realised.

GRACE. I realise –

STUDENTS 9, 10 *and* 11. Grace had lost the plot.

GRACE. The IT wants to be heard.

*

STUDENTS 12 *and* 13.

STUDENT 12. Grace?

GRACE. The IT hisses and spits and growls.

STUDENT 12. Grace Freemantle?

GRACE. When I speak, the IT cracks through all my words.

STUDENT 12. Grace Freemantle in 11F?

GRACE. I stop speaking.

STUDENT 12 *looks at* STUDENT 13. *They burst out laughing.*

*

SAM. Me and Grace just got each other. Right from the start, that first day that we met in Year 1. She was really kind... is really... was... is, yeah... She always made me feel like it's okay to be me. And a lot of times, I feel horrible being me. I hate my body.

GRACE. I keep my mouth shut.

SAM. And when I look around me, I see loads of other people hating their bodies too and their bodies look just fine to me.

GRACE. I keep my mouth shut.

SAM. After school we'd always go to Grace's house and make macaroni cheese, which was our thing. We love... loved macaroni cheese.

GRACE. I keep my mouth shut.

SAM. But then she just, kind of disappeared. Not literally. She was still around, but she wasn't, if you know what I mean. She stopped communicating.

GRACE. I keep my mouth shut.

SAM. She started staying after school in the library and getting the bus home when everyone was long gone.

GRACE. I keep my mouth shut.

SAM. She stopped asking me to come over to her house. She stopped texting me. She stopped talking to me. She stopped everything. Snapchat, WhatsApp, Insta, TikTok. All of it. Everything. Finished.

GRACE. I keep my mouth shut.

SAM. I missed her. (*Beat.*) I miss her. (*Beat.*) One day at school, I said to her, 'Do you want to walk home together today?'

GRACE. I keep my mouth shut.

SAM. I said, 'We can walk home and then go to yours to make macaroni cheese.'

GRACE. I keep my mouth shut.

SAM. She didn't say anything. I took a big breath and I asked her what I've been wanting to ask her for weeks. (*Beat.*) 'Grace, don't you like me any more?'

GRACE. I keep my mouth shut.

SAM. And she didn't say anything.

GRACE. I keep my mouth shut.

*

GRACE. I am at home. I am standing at the kitchen sink getting a drink of water. The IT is resting. It occasionally rolls over and stretches along my abdomen. My mum comes in and puts on the radio to listen to the news.

NEWSREADER. Yesterday afternoon a fourteen-year-old boy was stabbed to death in North London.

GRACE. The IT tenses.

NEWSREADER. Witnesses say they saw the victim being chased by a group of three or four other youths.

GRACE. I don't know why, but I go right up to where the radio is.

NEWSREADER. The victim is thought to have run into a local shop for help.

GRACE. Suddenly, without warning, the IT moves up over my shoulder and squeezes into my arm. I turn up the radio. A local mother comes on.

LOCAL MOTHER. We're scared for our children.

GRACE. There is a sharp pain in my hand.

LOCAL MOTHER. We're scared when our children go to school.

GRACE. There's a tiny cut in my hand.

LOCAL MOTHER. We're scared when our children are out of sight.

GRACE. There's blood in the palm of my hand.

LOCAL MOTHER. We need someone to do something.

GRACE. There's something sticking out of the palm of my hand.

LOCAL MOTHER. He was fourteen. Just a kid.

GRACE. It looks like a thorn from a rose, but it's bright blue.

LOCAL MOTHER. That poor boy lying in his own blood.

GRACE. It's a claw.

LOCAL MOTHER. Why is no one doing anything?

GRACE. There is a claw sticking out of the palm of my hand.

LOCAL MOTHER. Why does no one care?

GRACE. I try to push the claw back in with my fingertip.

LOCAL MOTHER. That boy, terrified, screaming, knowing he's going to die.

GRACE. It won't go back in.

LOCAL MOTHER. Screaming for his mum.

GRACE. I go to the bathroom. I close the bathroom door. I take my shoe off.

LOCAL MOTHER. The fifth teenage boy to be killed round here.

GRACE. I hit the palm of my hand with the shoe like a hammer.

LOCAL MOTHER. And no one in charge seems to give a toss.

GRACE. The claw resists.

LOCAL MOTHER. That poor boy.

GRACE. The claw resists

LOCAL MOTHER. That poor poor boy

GRACE. I wrap gaffer tape around my hand.

*

STUDENT 14. Remember those lessons we had in history about the Middle East?

STUDENT 15. Yeah, boring.

STUDENT 14. With Mr Logan.

STUDENT 15. Yeah, dickhead.

STUDENT 14. Remember that test?

STUDENT 15. Yeah, easy.

STUDENT 14. When I was sitting next to Grace Freemantle?

STUDENT 15. Yeah, Freemental.

STUDENT 14. That's not nice.

STUDENT 15. True though.

STUDENT 14. Grace didn't answer one question in that test. She just sat there staring at the paper. She didn't even pick up her pen.

STUDENT 15. Maybe it was hard to pick up a pen with them woolly gloves on.

—

Joke.

STUDENT 14. That's not funny.

—

I don't think you should joke about her.

—

I don't think we should be making jokes about her.

—

I wouldn't like it if that happened to me and everyone –

STUDENT 15. Okay, okay. God.

Silence.

STUDENT 14. You know that photo of that little boy in Syria who was bombed?

—

When Grace saw that photo, she started to shake.

GRACE. The pain inside is...

CHORUS. A four-year-old boy sits on an orange chair. The chair is too big for him. Aleppo is bombed. The little boy is dusty from the exploded buildings. His hair is matted and chalky. One side of his face is covered in blood. The little boy sits neatly with his hands on his knees. He is silent and traumatised.

GRACE. The pain inside me is unbearable.

STUDENT 14. The whole desk started moving. Her whole body was shaking. I asked her if she was alright, but she didn't say anything. I tried to get Mr Logan's attention, but Grace looked at me in a way that, I don't know, made me feel that I shouldn't.

—

I should have told Mr Logan.

—

Maybe if I'd told Mr Logan then that thing in PE would never have happened.

—

It's obvious that something was going on with her.

—

She was in trouble and I didn't do anything. I should have done something.

STUDENT 15. Yeah.

STUDENT 14. Do you think?

STUDENT 15. Yeah. No. I don't know.

*

GRACE. I can't stop watching the news. I can't stop reading the news. I can't stop listening to the news. I don't want to. I shut my eyes. I cover my ears.

CHORUS. Food banks, cyclones, arms dealing, police brutality, celebrity make-up brands, missing women, government corruption, self-harm in prisons, plutocrats,
another
racist
murder.

George Floyd.

Say His Name.

George Floyd.

TV reunions, domestic violence, white supremacy, luxury yachts, suicide in young men, immigration detention centres, an epidemic of loneliness, wildfires raging across countries, raging raging raging raging –

GRACE. The IT crawls up through my chest. Its spiky head reaches my throat.

It wriggles up. (*Coughs*.) Its beak is stuck in the back of my throat. (*Coughs*.) Its beak opens like a baby bird wanting to be fed. It speaks. The IT speaks and it says, 'What is next?'

CHORUS. Extinction.

GRACE. I gulp, I gulp and I gulp it back until it is forced back down my throat, back down into my body, pulsing and vibrating back in the pit of my stomach. I put tape over my mouth.

*

STUDENT 16. Grace, man, Grace.

STUDENT 17. Yeah, Grace, man.

STUDENT 16. With the – (*Mimes gloves*.) and the – (*Motions to head*.)

STUDENT 17. Balaclava.

STUDENT 16. Nah, that's a pastry thing.

STUDENT 17. No, that's –

STUDENT 16. Nah, that's a Turkish Greek Arabic pastry thing.

STUDENT 17. That's baklava.

STUDENT 16. Nah that's definitely… Oh yeah, you're right.

STUDENT 17. My Year 4 teacher used to bring baklava in at the end of term. Sick.

GRACE. I cover my face.

STUDENT 16. So one day Grace comes to school wearing this…

STUDENT 17. Balaclava.

STUDENT 16. And it wasn't winter or nothing.

GRACE. They all take the piss. I don't give a shit.

STUDENT 16. I don't know how she got away with it. They put me in isolation when I wore my trainers two days in a row and I had a proper reason. My school shoes were getting fixed.

STUDENT 17. Yeah, I remember.

STUDENT 16. Just cos I didn't have a note.

STUDENT 17. Yeah, I remember.

STUDENT 16. It was an extreme reaction.

STUDENT 17. Yeah, I remember.

GRACE. At break time, I go to the toilet, I take my clothes off. I watch the IT move around inside my body, bumping and poking and pushing at my skin. It has grown so big. A long low growl rumbles through my blood, muscle and gristle. What is next?

STUDENT 16. And then Grace Freemantle comes in wearing her baklava.

STUDENT 17. Balaclava.

GRACE. What is next?

STUDENT 16. And she's allowed to wander round willy-nilly wearing her…

STUDENT 17. Balaclava.

STUDENT 16. Happy as Larry in her…

BOTH…. Balaclava – (*High-five/fist-bump.*)

GRACE. What is next?

*

CHORUS. Rich people hunt giraffes and tigers and lions and rhinos. Rich people follow the animals in Jeeps. They stalk them and watch them and raise their guns as the giraffes and tigers and lions and rhinos stop for a drink at the river in the burning sun. Bang.

*

GRACE. I fall asleep on the floor of my bedroom.

CHORUS. There are people in a camp in Calais. There are people in a camp in Kos. There are people in a camp in Bangladesh –

GRACE. My dreams are infiltrated.

CHORUS. They've run away from their own countries.
They've run away from war and terror and hunger.

GRACE. My dreams are infiltrated.

CHORUS. The people used to live in peace with grandparents
and friends and neighbours.

GRACE. I wake up.

CHORUS. They used to sip tea and break bread with smiles and
love. They used to bicker about parking spaces and the music
that next door played at 3 a.m.

GRACE. I have a terrible pain just below my belly button.

CHORUS. They used to sing the old songs and dance to the
new songs and laugh about silly things like the way
Grandma eats pomegranates.

GRACE. There is a trickle of blood.

CHORUS. The children used to go to school and learn their
one-two-threes. Then guns and bombs and helicopters
arrived.

GRACE. There is a rip in my stomach.

CHORUS. The women and men gathered up their children and
started to run. They travelled miles with their possessions on
their backs.

GRACE. I peel back the skin.

CHORUS. The women and children and men are not wanted in
the camps of Calais and Kos and Bangladesh.

GRACE. There is an eye.

CHORUS. They dream of home.

GRACE. A yellow eye.

CHORUS. They dream of Grandma eating her breakfast in the
pink light of the morning. They dream of banging on the
wall at 3 a.m. and shouting at their neighbour to turn his
music down.

GRACE. A bright-yellow eye.

CHORUS. There are women and children and men in a different type of camp in the South of France.

GRACE. A bright yellow eye with a thin black pupil.

CHORUS. They wake up in the morning and have croissants and jam and coffee. They stretch their legs and yawn into the glimmering sun.

GRACE. The IT blinks up at me.

CHORUS. They think about the day ahead, which will be full of giggles and sandcastles.

GRACE. We look at each other.

CHORUS. And swimming and suncream and cool bubbly drinks. 'Ah, this is the life,' they sigh, 'this is the life.'

GRACE. I think I know what it wants.

*

STUDENT 18. Grace. Yes. Grace. In PE. Fruit loop. One hundred per cent fruit loop.

*

SAM. It was after school and I'd been at science revision. I'd left my coat in the lab so I was running back to get it when I saw Grace in an empty classroom. She was there all on her own, sitting very still, very upright, very neat. She was staring into space. I went in and I said, 'Is everything okay, Grace?' But she didn't look at me. I moved closer to her. I saw something flicker in her eyes.

GRACE. The IT is flexing its wings.

SAM. I thought she was going to say something.

GRACE. Stretching its legs.

SAM. I touched her shoulder.

GRACE. Grooming its fur or its feathers or its scales.

SAM. She flinched and she got up.

GRACE. I can feel all of its muscles.

SAM. She moved to the door. I reached for her arm.

GRACE. I can feel its strength.

SAM. And I said, 'Grace, tell me what's happening.'

GRACE. I can feel its power.

SAM. She shrugged me off.

GRACE. It is preparing.

SAM. I grabbed hold of her blazer.

GRACE. It's nearly ready.

SAM. I grabbed her and she turned round and she pushed me so hard that I fell over. I hit my head on the side of a desk and it started to bleed.

GRACE. I am scared.

SAM. I said, 'Look what you've done.'

GRACE. I am so scared.

SAM. And she turned around and walked away. And I shouted after her. I shouted, 'I hate you!'

GRACE. I am so so scared.

SAM. And that was the last time I saw her.

*

STUDENT 19. My auntie's friend knows Grace's neighbour and he told my auntie's friend that when Grace started wearing all those clothes that the teachers thought she had something wrong with her which meant she was cold all the time. Apparently Grace's parents contacted the school and said she had some condition. I don't know what that condition would be but it doesn't really matter because she didn't have any condition and her parents didn't contact the school either. It was Grace. Grace sent an email pretending to be them.

GRACE. The inside of me is heating up. I can hardly breathe. I can hardly move. I tape my whole body up to make a barrier. I wear a layer of clothes under my school uniform and an old puffa jacket over the top. My mouth is covered. My hands are covered. My head is covered. It cannot get out. I cannot let it get out.

STUDENT 19. My auntie's friend says that Grace's neighbour said that Grace's parents are really nice. He said they are 'switched on'. I think that means they know what's going on. Although they didn't seem to know what was going on with Grace and she's their daughter. Not that I think it's their fault. I don't tell my parents a bean about my life. They say, 'What happened at school today?' I say, 'Nothing.' They say, 'What are you doing in your bedroom?' I say 'Nothing.' They say, 'What are you looking at online?' I say, 'Nothing.' Grace's neighbour said Grace's parents are devastated. He said that they had no idea what was happening to her. That if only they'd known then that day in PE could have been avoided. They could have helped her or stopped it or I don't know, but they could have done something, which I'm sure is true. Someone should've been able to do something to help her before… you know. Don't you think?

*

STUDENT 20. I was in PE when it happened. The whole thing was, like, total madness. It was a boiling hot day and we had a supply teacher. The supply teacher wanted us to run one hundred metres. I shouted out, 'That's against our human rights!' and everybody creased. I'm a joker, innit. Everyone was in shorts and T-shirts apart from Grace who was dressed in all her gear looking like a colossal nutter.

GRACE. Pulse.

STUDENT 20. Um, I'd like to take that back. She didn't look like a colossal nutter; she looked… unusual. Yeah, that's right, she looked unusual in her… unusual… apparel. Anyway, we were outside on the field, which was as dry as the savanna cos of the heatwave and we were all lined up to run the first race.

Grace was on the other side of me. The supply teacher woman blew a whistle and we all set off. No one could be arsed, so there was a lot of dawdling and chit-chat.

GRACE. Pulse.

STUDENT 20. The general lack of effort pissed the supply teacher off and she proper shouted at us.

SUPPLY TEACHER. You are supposed to be competing!

GRACE. The IT freezes.

SUPPLY TEACHER. Whoever's last gets a detention!

STUDENT 20. The supply teacher was a wild one. Everybody started running.

GRACE. The IT darts its head.

STUDENT 20. And then someone shouted something about Riley Miller.

STUDENT 21. Fastest Tits in the Borough!

STUDENT 20. And everyone started laughing.

GRACE. The IT clenches its jaw.

CHORUS. Six hundred and nine tears-of-laughter faces.

GRACE. The IT arches its scaly back. Its spikes flicker.

CHORUS. A hundred and ten green sick faces.

GRACE. The IT's claws retract and protract.

STUDENT 20. I finished the race and turned back to see if I was last, which I wasn't, which was surprising to me cos I usually am. Grace was way behind me, standing dead still in her lane. And the supply teacher was lining up the next race to go.

BARRISTER. What I want to know is, what are you doing to stand out from everyone here?

GRACE. The IT opens its beak and bares its teeth.

CHORUS. There are children and women and men in an inflatable boat in the sea.

GRACE. The IT plunges and heaves and dives inside me.

STUDENT 20. The supply teacher spotted Grace and marched up to her and was all – (*Gesticulating*.) but Grace didn't even look at her.

MUM. Remember, it's your future.

GRACE. The IT whirls in a fever of blistering heat around my organs.

CHORUS. The waves are enormous.

STUDENT 20. The supply teacher was shouting her head off, right in Grace's face and Grace was standing still as a statue, ignoring her, which was making the supply teacher apoplectic.

CHORUS. Hashtag Ditsy Bikinis! Hashtag easyJet!

GRACE. It twists my liver.

MUM. Grace, are you revising?

GRACE. It snaps at my kidneys.

CHORUS. There are people in a camp in Calais.

GRACE. It claws at my lungs.

STUDENT 20. Eventually, the supply teacher got fed up and stomped off back to the starting line to have a go at someone else.

CHORUS. There are people in a camp in Kos.

GRACE. It starts to shred my muscles.

STUDENT 20. Grace stayed where she was. In the middle of the lane in the middle of the track in the middle of the school field on a boiling hot day.

CHORUS. There are people in a camp in Bangladesh.

GRACE. You know when you see a dog digging? It's doing that to the soft flesh inside of me.

LOCAL MOTHER. The fifth teenage boy to be killed round here.

STUDENT 20. And the supply teacher started the next race. The runners pointed at Grace and the supply teacher motioned they should run round her.

LOCAL MOTHER. And no one in charge seems to give a toss.

GRACE. I am filling up with blood.

STUDENT 20. The girl who was running in Grace's lane looked a bit worried about the human obstacle and said something to the teacher who suddenly shouted:

STUDENT 20 *and* SUPPLY TEACHER. Just EFFING RUN!!!

STUDENT 20. And instead of cracking up with laughter or saying they were going to report her to the Headteacher, everybody just started to effing run.

CHORUS. The woman disappears under a crash of foam and bubbles.

GRACE. Its talons scratch up at my larynx. I cough up blood.

CHORUS. Food banks, cyclones, arms dealing.

GRACE. It crushes my heart.

STUDENT 20. But the girl who was running in Grace's lane veered so far into the other lane that she tripped up whoever, who tripped up whoever, and so on until there was a whole pile of them and they all started cracking up.

CHORUS. Rich people hunt giraffes and tigers and lions and rhinos.

GRACE. It snaps off my ribs and pushes through. The pain…

CHORUS. Bang.

STUDENT 20. And we all started cracking up.

MS JARVIS. The earth's climate is changing at an unprecedented speed.

GRACE. The pain is…

STUDENT 20. Everybody was cracking up.

CHORUS. The little boy is dusty from the exploded building.

GRACE. It burrows its face up through my throat.

STUDENT 20. It was so funny.

CHORUS. Another racist murder.

GRACE. I gulp down.

CHORUS. Terror

GRACE. I gulp down.

CHORUS. Another racist murder.

GRACE. I gulp down.

STUDENT 20. We were literally rolling around on the floor in hysterics.

GRACE. It forces my mouth open.

CHORUS. The children used to go to school to learn their one-two-threes. Then guns and bombs and helicopters arrived.

STUDENT 20. And suddenly there was this noise. Like someone was being attacked.

GRACE. Its head rams my teeth.

CHORUS. Hashtag bring on the summer!

STUDENT 20. And we looked at the 'just effing run' supply teacher and it wasn't her.

GRACE. My teeth shatter and crumble from my mouth.

LOCAL MOTHER. That poor boy. That poor poor boy.

STUDENT 20. The supply teacher was staring at the third lane of the running track.

GRACE. My cheeks split as the IT hauls itself out of me.

STUDENT 20. All our eyes swivelled to where she was looking. It was Grace.

DAD. Your behaviour is completely inappropriate for a young lady.

GRACE. Its scaly feet kick at the sides of my throat.

STUDENT 20. Grace was standing in exactly the same position.

CHORUS *sings a line from song in previous scenes.*

GRACE. It uses my windpipe as a launch-pad.

STUDENT 20. But her mouth was open.

MUM. It's your future!

GRACE. It wrestles itself out of me. It is slick and wet, covered in blood and pus. Its tail slaps my face as it launches itself into the sky.

STUDENT 20. Her head was tilted right back.

MS JARVIS. We see crop failure and starvation.

GRACE. Its enormous wings unfurl mid-air with blast and yellow and clash.

STUDENT 20. Her face turned up to the sky.

MS JARVIS. Desertification and forced migration.

GRACE. The wings are bright green and iridescent.

STUDENT 20. And her mouth wide open.

CHORUS. annabeauty! I want your bag! I want your life!

GRACE. Flecks of fire spin off its scaly body like a Catherine wheel.

STUDENT 20. The noise was unbelievable.

CHORUS. The boat upturns.

GRACE. It stinks of fire and demons and rupture and storm.

STUDENT 20. The noise was so loud.

GRACE. The sky is filled with red and orange and clot and guts.

CHORUS. The boy's hair is matted and chalky.

STUDENT 20. It was frightening.

GRACE. The whole world heats up.

MUM. It's your future!

GRACE. The adults in charge run for safety.

STUDENT 20. The noise that was coming from her was so frightening.

GRACE. It Is all their fault.

CHORUS. Wildfires raging across countries, raging raging raging –

GRACE. The IT is coming for them.

STUDENT 20. I'll never forget that.

GRACE. The IT blinks its bright-yellow eyes. The earth shudders.

CHORUS. Extinction.

GRACE. It opens its beak, full of howl.

STUDENT 20. She was…

CHORUS. Bang.

GRACE. It cuts out the sunlight

STUDENT 20. She was…

CHORUS. Bang.

GRACE. We descend into darkness.

CHORUS. Bang.

GRACE. Full of fury and brilliance –

STUDENT 20. She was…

CHORUS. Bang.

GRACE. And fever and magnificence –

STUDENT 20. She…

CHORUS. Bang.

GRACE. The IT stops the world with a –

STUDENT 20. She…

GRACE *roars*.

*

STUDENT 22. They tried to get Grace Freemantle off the school field, but she wouldn't go. It was awful. Eventually, three teachers carried her off. They took her to the medical room. Her parents arrived. They put a blanket around her and walked her to their car. Her mum was asking her loads of questions, but Grace wasn't saying anything. She looked exhausted. Her whole body was sagging and, at one point, she stumbled and they had to catch her and hold her up. She didn't come back to school. I don't know where she went. No one knows where she went. Even her best friend, Sam, doesn't know. No one told us anything. Everyone has different theories about why it happened; exam pressure, drugs, eating disorders, boy trouble, girl trouble, friend trouble, parent trouble. I don't join in. I don't say anything. When they're all gossiping and giggling and talking in whispers, I don't say one word. Because when they all saw Grace Freemantle lose her shit on the PE field that day, when they all saw her open her mouth and scream and scream and scream up at the sky, I saw something different. I probably shouldn't say this. (*Pause*.) I saw it crawl out of her mouth and open its wings and cover the sky. I saw it shower flames of yellow and gold and rust all over us. I saw it open its beak and roar. I saw what was inside her, the fury, the fury, the blood, the gore, the fury. I saw it, because it's in me too. I know it is, I can feel it. It's just here…

I feel… a presence.
A gnawing.
A squirming.
It's small.
Like a cherry pip.
Or a baby shrimp.
It is really small.

Whatever it is.
But it's here.
It is definitely here.

Optional: GRACE *watches* STUDENT 22. *She offers her hand.*

The End.

www.nickhernbooks.co.uk

facebook.com/nickhernbooks

twitter.com/nickhernbooks